D0856502

ALZHEIMER'S DISEASE

ALZHEIMER'S DISEASE
The Silent Epidemic

Julia Frank

Lerner Publications Company   Minneapolis

ACKNOWLEDGMENTS: The photographs in this book are produced through the courtesy of: p. 8, copyright © Eric Kamp, Phototake; p. 12, copyright © Ann Chwatsky, Phototake, pp. 22, 59, Dr. Elias E. Manuelidis, Yale University School of Medicine; pp. 35, 44, 64 (top), General Electric Company; p. 62, Computer Technology & Imaging, Inc.; p. 64 (bottom), Dr. Robert Lufkin, UCLA Medical Center; p. 73, copyright © Bob Sacha, Phototake

Library of Congress Cataloging in Publication Data

Frank, Julia.
    Alzheimer's disease.

    Includes index.
    Summary: Explains the progressive brain disorder Alzheimer's disease, gives case histories of victims, and describes the problems faced by their families.
    1. Alzheimer's disease. [1. Alzheimer's disease] I. Title.
RC523.F73   1985   618.97′683   84-23320
ISBN 0-8225-1578-4 (lib. bdg.)

Manufactured in the United States of America

1 2 3 4 5 6 7 8 9 10 94 93 92 91 90 89 88 87 86 85

*For Marguerite
who would have written this book
had she been able*

Contents

SARAH

Like many young people, Ann and Peter were very fond of their one living grandmother. Grandma Sarah, their father's mother, made delicious gingerbread full of raisins and told fascinating stories about her life in Europe before she came to the United States as a young woman. Sarah lived with Peter, Ann, and their parents, and she often took her grandchildren on shopping expeditions and to the movies. The children felt lucky to have their grandmother with them.

Sarah was healthy and active at age 64, but in recent years, she had become forgetful. Sometimes she made her famous gingerbread and didn't remember to put in the raisins. Once she lost her glasses and looked all over the house for them until Ann noticed that they were on Sarah's head, pushed back into her hair. Everyone, including Sarah, laughed about her lapses of memory.

As Sarah grew older, however, her memory seemed to get much worse. She not only misplaced things but also forgot the names of friends or the characters on television programs that she watched frequently. Ann, Peter, and their parents were becoming concerned about Sarah's condition. Sarah too seemed worried about her failing memory, although she often became upset if someone suggested that anything was wrong. On one occasion when she couldn't find her watch, she denied losing it and insisted that a thief must have gotten into the house and taken it.

As Sarah's mental confusion got steadily worse, her relatives became really concerned. Finally, after Sarah wandered away from the family and got lost while visiting a shopping center, her son and daughter-in-law insisted that she go to the family doctor to find out what was causing her mental problems. The doctor tested Sarah and asked many questions about her habits and general health. Then he made his diagnosis: he believed that Sarah had Alzheimer's disease.

No one in the family had heard of this illness, and they were shocked and frightened when the doctor described it to them. He told them that Alzheimer's was a degenerative disease of the brain for which there is no known cure. Sarah would never get any better; her condition would only worsen until she was unable to function mentally or to take care of herself. The Sarah that they had known and loved—the alert, active woman who had played such an important role in their lives—would soon be gone, and she would never return.

THE SILENT EPIDEMIC

Today this same painful scene is taking place in doctors' offices throughout the United States and in other parts of the world. More and more people are receiving the sad news that older members of their families — grandparents, parents, aunts, uncles — have Alzheimer's disease. Based on recent estimates, about five percent of the American population over 65 suffers from this incurable illness. In the mid-1980s, at least 2 million people were condemned to live the last years of their lives in helplessness and mental disability.

By the end of the century, the number of victims of Alzheimer's disease is expected to increase dramatically. As Americans live longer and the birth rate remains low, the size of the population over 65 is steadily growing. By the year 2000, as many as 4 million of these older citizens may be victims of Alzheimer's disease. No wonder that doctors and researchers talk about a "silent epidemic" of the illness.

The epidemic is described as silent because so little is known about Alzheimer's disease, either by the public or by medical experts. Although the illness was identified in 1906 by a German neurologist named Alois Alzheimer (ALTS-hi-mer), it was not until the 1960s that doctors began to study it seriously and to diagnose it in their patients. Before that time, many people believed that confusion and trouble with memory were a "natural" part of growing old. Such mental disability was often called *senility* and considered a sad but unavoidable condition suffered by those who were unlucky enough to live long lives.

Today scientists believe that while older people may have some problems with their memories, severe memory loss and confusion are not normal. Instead, they are symptoms of diseases that cause physical damage in the brain. One of the most common of these ailments is Alzheimer's disease.

Although much remains unknown about this destructive illness, medical researchers are studying it intensely and more is being learned each day about its causes and symptoms. Recent advances in basic research on the brain have also helped in increasing our understanding of Alzheimer's disease. In addition to research on the causes and possible cures of the disease, much attention has been given to the care needed by Alzheimer's victims and the problems faced by family members who must provide this care.

This book will take a look at all these aspects of Alzheimer's disease as well as presenting case histories of some of the victims and their families.

THE EARLY STAGES

*"I used to be a physician. I used to drive
a car. I don't sing anymore. I probably
won't sing again.... I've lost a kingdom.
...I've lost everything."*

These heartbreaking words were spoken by a woman in the early stages of Alzheimer's disease. They reflect the gradual loss of mental and physical abilities that is typical of this devastating illness. Alzheimer's is a progressive disease, beginning with minor symptoms that may seem unimportant, such as Sarah's losing her glasses or forgetting ingredients in a recipe. Over a period of years, however, the symptoms become increasingly worse until the victim of the disease is robbed of all ability to function normally.

Like Sarah, most people with Alzheimer's disease first have problems with *short-term* or *recent memory.* They have trouble remembering things about the present or the recent past—where they put their glasses or watches, whether they mailed a birthday card to a friend.

Of course, these are problems that most of us have from time to time, but older people are particularly subject to lapses in recent memory. Although they may remember vividly events from the distant past, like Sarah's memory of her life as a girl in Europe, they have difficulty recalling things they have learned recently.

Frequently, such memory problems are temporary, caused by fatigue or a period of ill health. They may also be part of the mild loss of intellectual ability that often comes with age. Lapses of memory are not *always* signs of Alzheimer's or other brain diseases, as we can see in the case of Josephine:

Josephine's daughter noticed that her 70-year-old mother was becoming absent-minded and irritable. Concerned about her mother's mental state, she took her to a doctor, who could find nothing seriously wrong. The doctor advised the family to wait and see what happened.

While Josephine's memory did not improve, it did not get much worse. Josephine learned to cope with her problem by writing notes to herself and asking family members to remind her of things. Five years after her visit to the doctor, the 80-year-old woman was still alert and functioning well. She became irritable at times, but these moods passed and she soon returned to her usual cheerful self.

If Josephine had had Alzheimer's disease, her mild memory loss would not have stayed the same over a period of years. It would have gotten worse, progressing from occasional forgetfulness to more serious forms of mental confusion.

During the next stage of the disease, often called the early confusional stage, victims usually begin to have difficulty in following directions and finding their way around.

Sarah first experienced these problems when she visited the zoo with her grandchildren Peter and Ann. In order to find her way from one part of the zoo to another, Sarah had to read large maps posted on the gates. But she had such difficulty understanding the maps that she could not figure out how to get from the ape house to the elephant park. Finally, Ann had to ask a zookeeper for directions.

Sarah's confusion was made worse because the zoo was unfamiliar territory to her. At this stage in the disease, she had no problems in getting to and from the corner drugstore or the neighborhood supermarket. These were familiar places that she had visited often and knew well. Learning her way around new places or absorbing new information, however, was becoming more and more difficult.

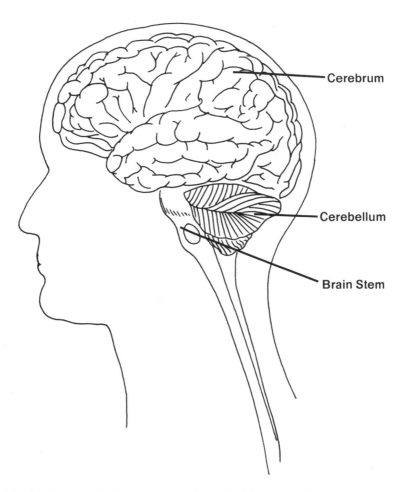

The human brain has three main parts. The massive *cerebrum* makes up two-thirds of the entire brain. It controls all the higher processes of human thought as well as the voluntary movements of the body. The main job of the *cerebellum* is to coordinate movements and control balance and posture. The *brain stem* connects the rest of the brain with the spinal cord and controls involuntary processes such as breathing.

Try to Remember

Sarah's symptoms clearly indicated that she was suffering from some kind of disturbance in the part of the brain that controls the processes of memory and learning. This complex physical system is still not well understood, but modern research has given us many new clues about its structure and function.

Scientists have been studying the operations of the human brain for at least 100 years, and they have gained solid information about many of its activities. We have learned that the brain controls every function of the body, from simple breathing to the most complex acts of artistic creativity. Extensive studies have been made of the way in which the brain receives and transmits information using a combination of electrical and chemical messages. Some of our knowledge of the brain's operation is quite detailed. For example, we know exactly what sections of the brain control the movements of particular body parts and which areas receive messages from the various sense organs such as the eyes or the ears.

Our knowledge of the structures that control memory and learning is not so precise, but researchers have been able to pinpoint certain regions of the brain that contribute to this vital function. We now know that the part of the brain called the *limbic system.* seems to play an important role in the processing and recording of new information.

CROSS SECTION OF BRAIN SHOWING
LOCATION OF LIMBIC SYSTEM

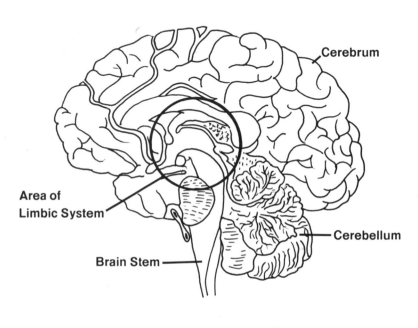

Cerebrum

Area of
Limbic System

Cerebellum

Brain Stem

Structures of
Limbic System
Affected by
Alzheimer's Disease

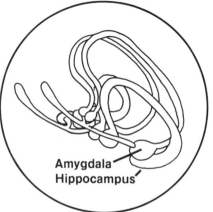

Amygdala
Hippocampus

Hidden under the cerebrum, the most massive part of the brain, the limbic system is made up of several structures with odd shapes and even odder names. Some of them, like the hypothalamus, control basic feelings like pleasure, hunger, fear, and anger. Others, like the *hippocampus* and the *amygdala,* seem to be involved in the process that allows information supplied by the senses to be recorded permanently in the brain.

Researchers believe that these parts of the limbic system help to transform recent memories, which are held in the brain very briefly, into permanent long-term memories. The hippocampus in particular seems to be vital to this process. Its role was first suggested by an operation performed in the 1950s on the brain of a young man suffering from epilepsy. Doctors thought that the man's severe epileptic seizures were being triggered by his hippocampus, so they surgically removed this small part of his brain. The patient's seizures disappeared, but so did his ability to remember anything for longer than a few minutes. Although his memories of the past were unchanged, he was completely unable to form any new long-term memories.

People in the early stages of Alzheimer's disease do not experience such a drastic loss of mental ability, but their problems with learning and remembering new things seem to be related to a similar cause. While they have not lost their memory-processing centers, they have usually suffered physical damage to these parts of their brains.

This damage is in the form of *lesions*, abnormal changes in the brain cells themselves. The lesions caused by Alzheimer's disease can be seen clearly only when an autopsy is performed on the brain of a deceased victim. (Sometimes they can be detected in the brains of living victims by special kinds of medical techniques, which will be described later.) Some of the lesions take the form of *plaques*, patches of dead brain cells. Others form *neurofibrillary tangles*, twisted threads of protein found within cells.

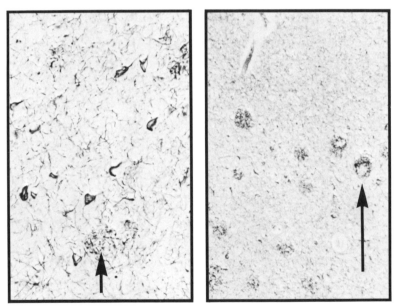

These photographs taken from microscopic slides of brain tissue show the plaques (left) and neurofibrillary tangles (right) that destroy the brain cells of Alzheimer's victims.

A few such abnormalities are usually found in the brains of most older people, but in Alzheimer's victims, they are much more numerous. Moreover, the lesions are concentrated in the limbic system and other parts of the brain connected with memory and learning. Their presence apparently interferes with the normal functioning of the brain cells in these areas, causing the symptoms of memory loss typical of Alzheimer's disease.

An autopsy on the brain of an Alzheimer's victim reveals the final stage in the formation of lesions and the destruction of cells. Confusion and problems with memory like those first experienced by Sarah are signs that the disease has just begun its relentless attack on the brain.

THE DISEASE PROGRESSES

*"I think that I am getting better, and
all the time I'm getting worse.... The
days go so slow for me."*

After suffering through the early stages of Alzheimer's disease, Sarah and other victims have no-
where to go but down. As the lesions in their brains
increase in number, their problems with memory and
learning become worse. They find it increasingly
difficult to deal with new information or new situations
and to make appropriate decisions. Because of these
problems, people in this late confusional stage of the
disease may begin to withdraw into themselves and
lose interest in the world around them. They may even
show signs of losing some part of their long-term
memory.

As her disease progressed, Sarah exhibited many of these worsening symptoms. Because of her impaired mental ability, she was no longer able to keep an accurate record of the checks she wrote and she began overdrawing her checking account frequently. Finally, her son had to take over control of Sarah's financial affairs, even though she greatly resented this loss of independence.

Peter and Ann knew that something was seriously wrong with their grandmother, and they noticed it particularly when she was telling them stories about her past life. Sarah still enjoyed talking about her girlhood in Europe, but now she had trouble remembering exactly what had happened or what the point was that she was trying to make. Sometimes Sarah's stories became so rambling and confused that the children couldn't follow them at all. When this happened, they sat in embarrassed silence, unable to look at their grandmother or each other.

The family noticed another significant change in Sarah's behavior during a presidential election that took place about three years after her symptoms first appeared. Sarah had always had strong views on politics, but now she did not seem to know much about the candidates or the issues they represented. The campaign speeches only confused her, and when the election took place, she did not bother to vote. It was the first time since she became a citizen that she had not participated in an election.

Because Sarah became so confused by new information and new situations at this stage in her illness, a steady, unchanging routine was very important to her. Once when her son and daughter-in-law went away on a two-week vacation, another relative came to stay with her and the two children. During this period, Sarah's confusion got much worse. One day, she forgot what season it was and put on a winter coat, even though it was hot outside.

When her son and his wife returned and the family routine was reestablished, Sarah became calmer and less confused. This improvement was not lasting, however. As time passed, the damaging effects of Alzheimer's disease on Sarah's brain were more and more evident.

Spreading Damage in the Brain

The physical damage caused by Alzheimer's disease affects many parts of that complex organ, the human brain. Autopsies have shown lesions not only on the structures of the limbic system but also on parts of the *cerebral cortex.* The cortex, the thin, wrinkled upper layer of the cerebrum, is one of the most important areas in the human brain. It is in this region that all the processes we call "thinking" seem to take place. Interpreting the messages of the senses, making plans and decisions, putting thoughts into words—these

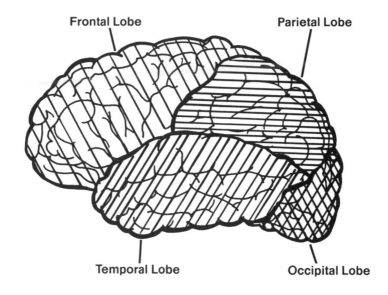

Frontal Lobe   **Parietal Lobe**

Temporal Lobe   **Occipital Lobe**

The cerebrum and its wrinkled outer layer, the cortex, are divided into two hemispheres, or halves. Each hemisphere has four major lobes formed by deep grooves in the surface of the cortex.

and other complex functions are the responsibility of the brain cells in the cortex.

The structure of the human cortex is extremely complicated, and many parts of it are not yet clearly understood. Researchers have gained the most information about two sections or bands known as the *motor cortex* and the *sensory cortex*. Cells in these two narrow strips running through the middle of the cortex are responsible for controlling voluntary movements and receiving messages from nerves in various parts of the body. The visual cortex, located in

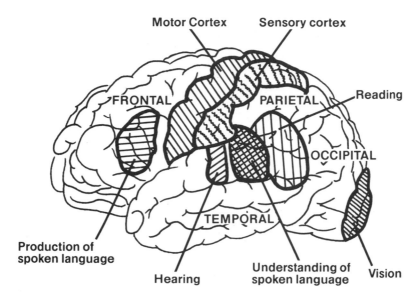

Motor Cortex   **Sensory cortex**

FRONTAL   PARIETAL   Reading

OCCIPITAL

TEMPORAL

Production of
spoken language

Hearing   Understanding of
spoken language   Vision

Some areas of the human cortex have very specific functions.
For example, the left hemisphere (shown above) contains
several important centers that control speech and language.
Both hemispheres also include large areas whose functions
are not as well known.

the occipital lobes at the back of the cerebrum, makes
it possible for us to see the world around us. Another
special section of the cortex is responsible for hearing.

The amazing complexity of human speech and
language is also under the control of brain cells in the
cortex. Researchers have identified several specific
areas that share this task. One area transforms the
sounds picked up by the ears into recognizable patterns
of words, while another produces speech. Ability to
recognize written language is controlled by another
part of the cortex.

Although some areas of the cortex have been mapped precisely, the functions of other areas are not as well known. Many of these undefined regions seem to be involved in thinking, planning, and retaining memories. Scientists group them under the name *association cortex* because of their apparent involvement in these sophisticated mental activities.

We have some clues about what goes on in various parts of the association cortex that are particularly helpful in understanding Alzheimer's disease. Experiments seem to show that the *frontal lobes* may be the areas of the cortex responsible for making plans and putting ideas in sequential order. Victims of Alzheimer's disease are often found to have many lesions in the frontal lobes of their brains. Because of these abnormal brain cells, people like Sarah gradually lose the ability to think clearly or to plan ahead. Sarah's difficulty in going through the step-by-step process of a recipe could have been an early sign of damage to her frontal lobes.

The part of the association cortex located on the *parietal lobes* also shows severe damage in many Alzheimer's victims. These areas of the cortex play a role in our ability to tell right from left and to understand our relationship to our surroundings. Damage to the parietal lobes may cause Alzheimer's victims to become confused and lose their way easily as Sarah did. The ability to make calculations also seems to be associated with the parietal lobes. Sarah's difficulty in balancing her checking account was another sign of the disease's effect on this part of her brain.

One of the most important jobs of the association cortex may be to serve as a storage place for long-term memories. Some scientists think that the *temporal lobes* in particular are areas where these memories are preserved in brain cells that have been chemically changed in some way. Lesions on the temporal lobes or in other areas of the association cortex may damage this storage system, destroying the knowledge of the past that is so important to normal human thought and planning.

Diagnosing Alzheimer's Disease

By the time that an Alzheimer's victim has reached the late confusional stage of the disease, relatives and friends have usually become well aware of the person's mental problems. Like Sarah's family, they will probably consult a doctor to find out what is causing the disturbing symptoms.

Unfortunately, Alzheimer's is not an easy disease to recognize or diagnose. Its symptoms are similar to other illnesses affecting the brain as well as to mental disorders like depression. Doctors usually classify symptoms such as mental confusion, loss of memory, and irrational behavior under the heading of *dementia*.

Alzheimer's is only one of several *dementing illnesses* that may attack older people.

The simplest way for a doctor to determine if a patient has Alzheimer's disease is to eliminate the possibility that he or she has any other dementing illness. Asking questions about the person's general health and present condition is one good way to begin such a diagnosis.

These are a few of the questions that Sarah's doctor asked when he first saw her: Did Sarah have high blood pressure? Did she drink large amounts of alcohol? Was she on any kind of medication that might make her confused?

Such questions were designed to pinpoint some of the health problems that might have been causing Sarah's dementia. For instance, if she had been taking medication to help her sleep, the doctor would want to find out how much of the drug she used and how it affected her system. Misuse of sedatives and other drugs can produce symptoms of dementia. Heavy use of alcohol can have the same effect.

One significant cause of dementia in older people is *stroke,* an interruption in the supply of blood going to the brain. When the doctor asked whether Sarah had high blood pressure, he was inquiring about a condition that often leads to strokes. Diabetes is another illness that can have the same results. Severe strokes cause sudden and massive brain damage, but a series of smaller strokes can produce gradual symptoms of dementia similar to those caused by Alzheimer's disease.

In diagnosing a demented patient, a physician always pays particular attention to the speed at which the symptoms developed. When a 60-year-old man named Simon came in for a medical exam complaining of confusion and forgetfulness, the doctor questioned the patient and his wife closely about when he had first experienced these symptoms. Simon's wife made it clear that he had been having trouble for only a few weeks. At work, Simon had difficulty getting organized and did not seem to notice when he made mistakes. His secretary found that he had to be reminded of his appointments, something that had not been necessary in the past. When Simon got lost driving home from work, both he and his wife knew that something was seriously wrong.

It did not take the doctor long to find out that several weeks before his symptoms appeared, Simon had been involved in a minor automobile accident. He had hit his head on the windshield and had been unconscious for about an hour. After spending a night in the hospital emergency room, Simon had gone home with nothing more than a headache and some dizziness.

When the doctor heard about Simon's accident, he immediately suspected that the head injury might be causing the symptoms of dementia. X-rays showed that this was the case. Blood clots created by the blow on the head were pressing against Simon's brain, disrupting its normal functioning. An operation was performed to drain the clots, and a month later, Simon was completely recovered.

An x-ray is only one of the standard medical procedures that a doctor might use in diagnosing a demented patient. Others include urinalysis and various kinds of blood tests. An electroencephalogram (EEG) is a more specialized test that can be used to measure the electrical activity in the brain itself. Irregularities in an EEG might indicate brain damage caused by a stroke or a tumor.

Unfortunately, none of these procedures can reveal the kind of brain damage resulting from Alzheimer's disease. In recent years, however, medical experts have developed a special x-ray technique that does show at least some of these changes. It is known as *Computerized Axial Tomography*, or *CAT scanning*. Unlike an ordinary x-ray, a CAT scan reveals details about the soft tissue of the brain. It can often show the shrinkage of brain tissue that results when cells are being destroyed by the lesions of Alzheimer's disease. CAT scans also reveal the buildup of fluid caused by the same destruction.

Although CAT scans can be helpful in diagnosing Alzheimer's disease, they are not very reliable. Sometimes a scan will show only slight brain damage in a patient who has severe symptoms of dementia. In other cases, a person with only minor symptoms will have a very abnormal scan. Because the results are

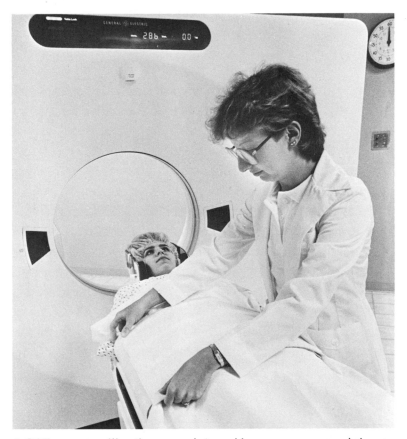

A CAT scanner like the one pictured here uses a special x-ray technique to reveal the soft tissue of the brain. CAT scans can show some of the damage caused by Alzheimer's disease, but they cannot be used alone to make a positive diagnosis of the illness.

so unpredictable, CAT scanning cannot be used alone to make a positive diagnosis of Alzheimer's disease. An even more advanced scanning technique, the PET scan, shows more promise but is not yet widely available. (PET scanning will be described in a later section of the book.)

Until more reliable methods are available, doctors will probably continue to diagnose Alzheimer's disease by a process of elimination. If an older person with symptoms of dementia does not have any other recognized dementing illness, then he or she is likely to have Alzheimer's disease.

Almost any other diagnosis would be preferable to someone suffering from dementia. There are positive steps that can be taken to help people who have blood clots or strokes, who are depressed or are misusing drugs. For an Alzheimer's victim, the outlook for the future is much more bleak. At present, there is no known treatment that can halt the progress of the disease or repair the brain damage it causes.

THE FINAL STAGE

*"What do I want? I don't want to
be here. I don't want to be here for
another birthday."*

In the final stages of Alzheimer's disease, the damage in the victim's brain causes widespread and serious disability. Memory loss, confusion, and other symptoms of dementia become so severe that the person has difficulty carrying out the tasks of everyday life. The victim's emotional state is also seriously affected, resulting in extreme changes in mood and temper. As Alzheimer's disease spreads to all parts of the brain, the afflicted person becomes completely bedridden and loses control over bodily functions.

Like other victims, Sarah became increasingly demented as the disease took its toll on her brain cells.

Five years after her memory loss began, she frequently did not recognize her granddaughter Ann when she came home on school vacations. On some days, Sarah asked repeatedly for her husband, Walter, not remembering that he had died long ago. In her confusion, she lost track of time completely and did not even know what year it was. Instead of sleeping at night, Sarah often got up and wandered around the house, rummaging through closets and drawers or trying to cook meals in the kitchen.

As the disease progressed, Sarah experienced increasing difficulty in doing things for herself. Even when a family member laid out her clothes, she had trouble putting them on. If the sleeve of a sweater was inside out, she could not figure out how to turn it right. Unless someone helped her, she often put her shoes on the wrong feet.

Although Sarah needed a great deal of help from her family, she did not always seem to appreciate their assistance. If someone corrected a mistake, she sometimes became angry or excited. She could also be very suspicious, accusing her relatives of cheating her or stealing her possessions. At other times, she seemed anxious or sad, withdrawn from the world around her.

Like Sarah's other symptoms, her extreme mood changes were signs of the growing damage in her brain. Lesions in her limbic system were affecting her ability to control emotions such as anger, fear, and sadness. Destruction of brain cells in the limbic system and in the cerebral cortex were also eating away at her memory. At this stage in the disease, she had not only lost the ability to form new memories but was also losing precious information from the past such as the memory of her granddaughter's face and name.

The problems that Sarah experienced in dressing herself probably stemmed from damage in the parietal lobes, the area in the cortex that governs a person's orientation or position in space. Because she no longer knew left from right, she could not tell which shoe went on which foot. This same confusion about proper position in space made it difficult for her to turn a reversed sleeve right side out.

Because of the spreading lesions in her brain, Sarah was becoming more and more helpless as time passed. Soon she would need the care and help of her whole family in order to get through a single day.

Caring for an Alzheimer's Victim

As Alzheimer's disease progresses through its final stages, victims like Sarah become increasingly unaware of what is happening to them. Their minds have been so damaged by the disease that they are no longer conscious of their disabilities or their strange behavior. As the suffering of the victim becomes less, however, the burden on relatives and friends grows.

Caring for a person in the last stages of Alzheimer's disease is an enormous job. Caretakers must act both as nurses and guardians, providing for the daily needs of their sick relative and protecting him or her from falls and other injuries. They must deal calmly and patiently with the victim's irrational and sometimes violent behavior. Finally, they must suffer the intense pain of seeing a well-loved parent or grandparent changed beyond recognition by the symptoms of the disease.

When Sarah began to require regular help with daily activities, Ann, Peter, and their parents felt the strain of these new demands on their time and energy. Each member of the family had his or her own responsibilities outside the home. Both young people were in school, Peter, in a local high school and Ann, at a college in a nearby town. Their parents had full-time jobs. Now the family members had to arrange their daily schedules to make sure that someone was always at home with Sarah. At night, their sleep was disturbed by Sarah's restless wandering around the house. Peter and his parents took turns getting up and trying to persuade her to return to bed.

One of the most distressing problems that the family faced was dealing with Sarah's *incontinence*—her increasing difficulty in controlling urination and bowel movements. They found it necessary to take her to the bathroom and make sure that she used the toilet. If this wasn't done, she sometimes wet or soiled herself, without seeming to be aware of it. Because of the damage in her brain, Sarah was like a child who does not know how to control its bodily functions. It was especially hard for Sarah's son to see his mother reduced to this condition.

Although the family found it difficult to provide all the care that Sarah needed, they were reluctant to look for outside help. Peter and Ann in particular were embarrassed by their grandmother's condition and her strange behavior and did not want anyone outside the family to know about it. But the family doctor urged Sarah's son and daughter-in-law to seek help for their own good and for Sarah's. Finally, they hired companions who came in from time to time to watch Sarah, making sure that she dressed and ate and did not injure herself. Although strangers at first, these helpers soon came to be regarded as part of the family. Their assistance helped to relieve the strain that the family members were experiencing.

Sarah's doctor also suggested that the family might ease their burden by meeting and talking with the relatives of other Alzheimer's victims. Sarah's son discovered that there was a support group in their community made up of such people. The family started going to meetings of the group, where they talked about their problems and got the advice of others in the same situation. This sharing of their difficulties and sorrows would prove very helpful to Sarah's family during the hard days ahead.

Despite Dedicated Care

Despite the dedicated care she received, Sarah lost ground over the next few years. She became unable to feed herself, even when food was put in front of her. Unless helped to a chair, she stayed in bed, and she spoke less and less. Finally, a time came when she hardly spoke at all. Frequently dropping into a light sleep, she seemed almost completely unaware of her surroundings.

It was very painful for the family to see Sarah this way. Though they still came to her room and tried to talk to her, she did not seem to recognize them. Sometimes they brought Sarah out to lie on the living room sofa when other relatives came to visit, but she was unaware of what was going on around her.

When Sarah was totally confined to bed and unable to do anything for herself, it became harder and harder to care for her. The family rented a hospital bed and hired some nurse's aides to help them, but if one of the aides couldn't come as scheduled, a family member had to stay home with Sarah. On one occasion when an aide was suddenly unable to come, Ann and her father were out of town and the other family members were sick with the flu. Despite his illness, Peter had to take care of his grandmother until another aide came on duty.

The difficulty in handling this emergency made the family realize that it was no longer practical or safe to keep Sarah at home. They visited several nursing homes that could provide the care Sarah needed and chose one in their neighborhood. Sarah was moved to the nursing home and the family came to visit her as often as they could.

About a year after she was moved to the nursing home, Sarah developed a lung infection brought on by her weakened physical condition. Despite treatment with antibiotics, the infection turned into a case of pneumonia that proved fatal. Sarah died peacefully in her sleep.

Like most people with Alzheimer's disease, Sarah died not as a direct result of damage to her brain but because of a secondary illness. Pneumonia or some other form of infection is often the immediate cause of death, but the ravages of Alzheimer's disease have made the person particularly vulnerable to such ailments.

Although Ann, Peter, and their parents were saddened by Sarah's death, they felt that the real Sarah had been gone from them for a long time. In the years after her death, they found that they remembered her not as the ill and helpless victim of a devastating disease but as the lively and loving woman she had once been.

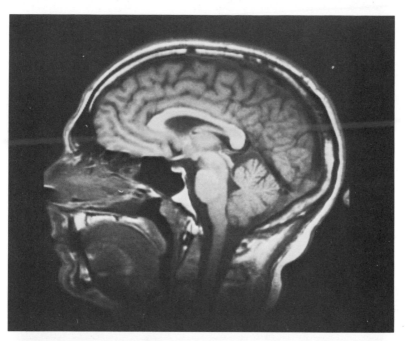
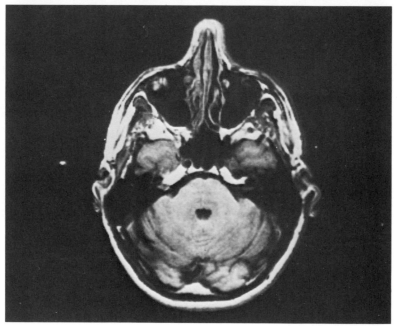

AUTOPSY OF A DISEASE

Human beings are usually afraid of the unknown, of disturbing things that happen without any apparent cause or reason. Alzheimer's disease is a frightening illness because it is so destructive, yet so little is known about its causes. What happens in the brain of a victim to create the lesions that produce such devastating symptoms? Why do some older people like Sarah develop the disease while others live out their final years mentally alert and in good health?

Scientists do not have any definite answers to these questions, but they do have some clues that may eventually lead to the unraveling of the mystery. One of the most promising of these clues concerns the destruction of brain cells that is typical of the disease. Many researchers believe that this destruction may be caused by a breakdown in the system of communication connecting the billions of cells that make up the human brain.

A Breakdown in Communications

There are two different kinds of cells in the brains of humans and other animals. One kind is the *neuron,* or nerve cell, usually made up of a cell body, many branching *dendrites,* and a long, tail-like *axon* that ends in a cluster of *terminal branches.* Neurons are the "thinking" cells of the brain, the ones that control all our memories, thoughts, feelings, and actions. They are also the cells damaged by Alzheimer's disease. Surrounding the neurons are billions of *glial cells;* they form a "glue" that supports the nerve cells and provides them with nourishment.

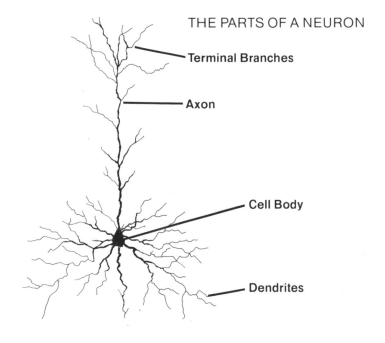

THE PARTS OF A NEURON

Terminal Branches

Axon

Cell Body

Dendrites

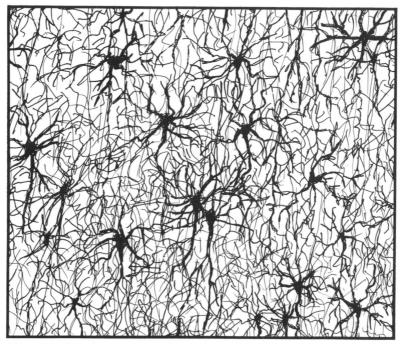

The 10 billion neurons of the human brain are joined together by a complex system of communication that uses both electrical and chemical messengers.

It has been estimated that the human brain contains at least 10 billion individual neurons. The amazing way in which these cells communicate with each other and with the neurons of the body's nervous system is one of the great discoveries of modern brain research.

Scientists have known for many years that the brain's communication system uses electrical impulses in some way. An electroencephalogram records and measures the waves of electrical energy that move constantly through a normal brain. It was only recently, however, that researchers learned about the role that chemicals play in connecting neurons with each other.

We now know that the brain and nervous system use both electricity and chemistry to transmit information, send commands, and perform all their other complex functions. The communication system works in this way: Information picked up by one of the body's sense organs is received by a neuron in the form of an electrical impulse. This impulse moves through the neuron's cell body and down the long axon. The axon's terminal branches are positioned close to but not quite touching the dendrites or body of at least one other nerve cell. The tiny space between the two cells, called a *synaptic cleft,* can be crossed only by a chemical bridge.

When the electrical impulse reaches the end of the axon, it triggers the release of chemicals known as *neurotransmitters.* The neurotransmitters move across the synaptic cleft and lock into special *receptors* located on the surface of the other neuron. Once it is received by the receptors, the chemical message is changed back into an electrical impulse, which is then transmitted to other neurons in the same manner.

By means of this unique communication system, the billions of neurons in the brain are connected to each other through amazingly complex pathways, or *circuits.* One neuron alone may be in touch with the axons or dendrites of 1,000 other neurons and be able to receive messages from thousands more. These connected neurons work together in receiving and interpreting information, in controlling the actions of the body, in storing memories. Because of the

HOW NEURONS COMMUNICATE WITH EACH OTHER

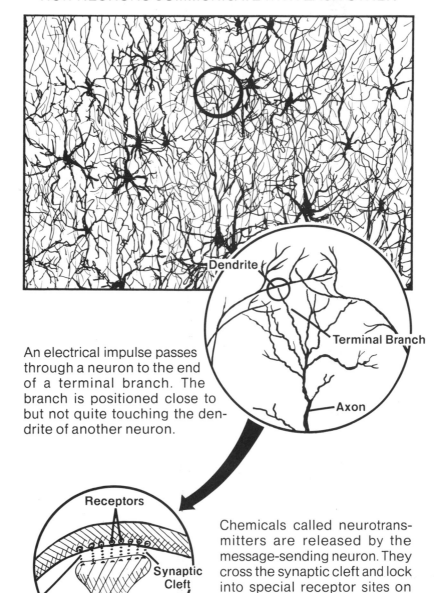

An electrical impulse passes through a neuron to the end of a terminal branch. The branch is positioned close to but not quite touching the dendrite of another neuron.

Dendrite

Terminal Branch

Axon

Receptors

Synaptic Cleft

Neurotransmitters

Chemicals called neurotransmitters are released by the message-sending neuron. They cross the synaptic cleft and lock into special receptor sites on the message-receiving neuron.

brain's neuron circuits, human beings are able to solve complicated problems, create great works of art, or construct elaborate plans for the future using millions of isolated pieces of information.

In recent years, scientists have discovered that all the neurons connected in a circuit usually produce and respond to the same kinds of neurotransmitters. Researchers have succeeded in isolating and identifying some of these chemical messengers, among them acetylcholine (ACH), norepinephrine (NE), serotonin (5-HT), and dopamine (DA). This information is not only of vital importance to brain research but has also been of great help in studying illnesses that affect nerve cells.

One major breakthrough has already been made in the treatment of Parkinson's disease, a nerve ailment causing loss of muscle control. Studies have shown that this disease is a result of damage in some of the dopaminergic brain circuits—those that use dopamine as a neurotransmitter. The symptoms of Parkinson's disease can be relieved by giving the patient drugs that replace the lost dopamine in the brain cells.

Could Alzheimer's disease also be related to problems in the brain's chemical circuits? Studies have indicated that this may be the case. Scientists have found at least two chemical circuits that are abnormal in Alzheimer's victims. The most important is the *cholinergic* circuit, which uses acetylcholine (ACH) as its primary neurotransmitter.

One of the main centers of cholinergic cells in the brain is an area known as the nucleus basilis. The cells in this region produce large amounts of ACH and use it in transmitting messages to other circuits of neurons. Tests on the brains of people who have had Alzheimer's disease show that they have abnormally low amounts of ACH in the nucleus basilis. There also seems to be a shortage of the enzymes that produce the chemical.

The cholinergic cells in the nucleus basilis have connections to many parts of the brain, including the limbic system and the frontal and parietal lobes of the cortex. Many researchers suspect that the shortage of ACH in the nucleus basilis affects communication among these cells, causing them to develop the lesions of Alzheimer's disease and eventually die.

To test this theory, they have tried to slow the progression of the disease by increasing the amount of ACH in the brains of victims. This is usually done by giving the patients large amounts of lecithin, a substance containing choline, one of the essential components of ACH. (The other component, acetyl, is found naturally in the brain.)

So far, these tests have not produced any significant results, although some slight improvement has been seen in a few of the people treated. It may be that there are simply not enough processing enzymes available to make ACH even when the supply of choline is

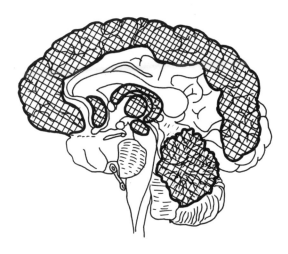

PARTS OF THE BRAIN USING ACETYLCHOLINE (ACH)
AS A PRIMARY NEUROTRANSMITTER

greatly increased. Further tests are underway using different methods of influencing the chemistry of the cholinergic circuits, and they may prove more successful. Many scientists believe that such tests and studies hold the most promise for the eventual discovery of an effective treatment for Alzheimer's disease.

Another chemical circuit that shows abnormality in the brains of Alzheimer's victims is the *adrenergic* circuit, made up of neurons that use norepinethrine (NE) as their main transmitter. (The word "adrenergic" comes from "noradrenaline," an older name for NE.) The locus ceruleus is an important center for these cells, and, like the nucleus basilis, it has connections with neuron circuits all over the brain. In some

Alzheimer's victims, the locus ceruleus has been shown to contain less than the normal amount of NE.

A recently discovered group of neurotransmitters called *brain peptides* may also be involved in the development of Alzheimer's disease. Some of these chemicals, especially vasopressin (VP) and enkephalin (ENK), seem to be concentrated in the parts of the brain that control memory. Tests on Alzheimer's victims have revealed decreased amounts of another peptide, somatostatin (SRIF), in areas of the cortex damaged by the lesions of the disease. This is another aspect of brain chemistry being studied by research scientists who are trying to solve the mystery of Alzheimer's disease.

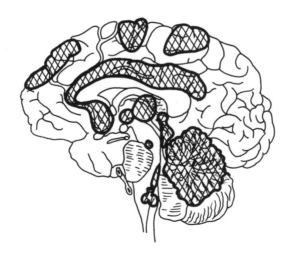

PARTS OF THE BRAIN USING NOREPINETHRINE (NE) AS A PRIMARY NEUROTRANSMITTER

The Roots of Alzheimer's Disease

Today many scientists seem confident that the destruction of brain cells in victims of Alzheimer's disease is produced by a breakdown in the chemical circuits of the brain. What they are not sure about is the underlying cause of this breakdown. Why do the cholinergic cells stop producing adequate amounts of ACH? Is it a genetic problem—some defect in the cells that a person is born with? Or is the abnormality perhaps caused by some kind of virus? There is support among scientists for both of these explanations.

Many researchers believe that there is probably some genetic factor in the development of Alzheimer's disease, although they are not sure how significant it is. They base their belief on statistics indicating that, under certain conditions, relatives of an Alzheimer's victim—people who share the same genes—are more likely to get the disease than those who do not have an afflicted relative. Studies show that the brothers and sisters of a person who develops Alzheimer's disease *under the age of 65* have a greater chance of becoming Alzheimer's victims themselves. (These studies have not been conducted over a long enough period of time to show whether children of victims have the same kind of risk.)

The hereditary factor in Alzheimer's disease is clearly associated with the age at which the illness develops. Some victims exhibit symptoms of dementia in their

40s and usually develop very severe cases of Alzheimer's disease. Statistics indicate that the younger the victim is at the onset of the illness, the more likely it is that relatives will also be victims. If someone develops Alzheimer's disease at the age of 40 (a fairly rare occurrence), then his or her sisters and brothers have a 40 percent chance of getting the disease, although not necessarily at the same early age. If the person did not become ill until age 60, however, then the risk falls to 20 percent.

Another indication that Alzheimer's disease might be hereditary is that families in which the disease occurs frequently have members with other known hereditary diseases. This is particularly true of Down's syndrome, a type of mental retardation known to result from defective genes. Families with Alzheimer's and Down's syndrome also tend to have members with leukemia and other forms of blood cancer that may be caused by genetic disorders.

The final piece in the genetic mosaic is the fact that people with Down's syndrome who live to be middle-aged almost always develop Alzheimer's disease. This collection of statistics suggests that some related hereditary factor may be involved in all these diseases. Researchers are conducting long-range studies to collect more information on this important subject.

Despite the strong evidence for some genetic element in the development of Alzheimer's disease, many cases occur in families that have no history of the disease at all. This suggests that the illness is not always inherited and that there must be many other factors involved in its development. It also means that even people who have several close relatives with Alzheimer's disease may not necessarily get it themselves.

In diagnosing the disease, however, it is helpful to know whether it has occurred in the family before. This is one of the reasons why an autopsy should be performed on anyone who has had a dementing illness. Only an examination of the brain will show whether the victim had Alzheimer's disease and whether his or her relatives may also be at risk.

The genetic explanation for Alzheimer's disease has many supporters, but other experts believe that the disease may be caused by a virus. They base their belief on the fact that several other brain diseases with similar symptoms are known to be caused by viral infections.

Two rare dementing diseases, kuru and Creutzfeldt-Jakob disease, produce plaques in the victims' brains that are very much like those caused by Alzheimer's disease. An animal disease called scrapie, found in sheep and goats, also produces similar lesions. All these diseases are caused by slow-acting viruses. Unlike the viruses that produce measles or the common cold, these viruses develop over a very long period of time. It can take years from the time the victim is infected until the symptoms of the disease appear.

Slow-acting viruses are very difficult to recognize.

They usually cannot be detected by a microscope, nor can they be grown in a laboratory like other viruses. The only way to prove that they exist and that they are the cause of a disease is to transmit them from one host to another. This is done by taking brain tissue from an infected person or animal and injecting it into a laboratory animal. If the test animal eventually develops the disease, then the existence of the disease-causing virus is established.

Kuru and Creutzfeldt-Jakob disease have been successfully transmitted in this way, but so far Alzheimer's disease has not. It may be that by the time a victim of Alzheimer's disease dies, the virus that originally caused the illness is no longer present in the brain. Another possibility is that not enough time has been allowed for the disease to develop in the test animal. Further studies may yet establish that a slow-acting virus is at least a factor in Alzheimer's disease as it is in similar dementing diseases.

In addition to the viral and genetic theories of the origins of Alzheimer's disease, researchers are investigating several other possible causes. Among them is the theory that the disease might be produced by some toxic, or poisonous, substance in the victim's environment.

At one time, the toxic theory seemed very promising because it explained one of the more puzzling symptoms of Alzheimer's disease—the presence of excessive amounts of the element aluminum in the brain tissue of some victims. The importance of this finding was reinforced by tests in which aluminum injected into the brains of laboratory rats produced neurofibrillary tangles similar to those of Alzheimer's disease. Based on such evidence, many researchers suspected that the disease might be a form of aluminum poisoning. Today, however, this theory does not have many supporters.

Recent studies have shown that while some Alzheimer's victims do have excessive aluminum in their brains, many others are completely free of this abnormality. Moreover, statistics indicate that people who are exposed to large amounts of aluminum in their environments do not seem to develop the disease more frequently than anyone else. These findings have led most scientists to conclude that there is no clear-cut evidence for considering Alzheimer's disease to be a form of aluminum poisoning. The presence of abnormal amounts of aluminum in the brains of some victims remains a mystery.

While aluminum poisoning does not seem to be a likely cause of Alzheimer's disease, it is possible that some other toxic agent may be involved. This is another area under intensive study.

In their search for the cause of Alzheimer's disease, some scientists have directed their attention to the body's immune system. They suspect that the illness may result from a malfunction of this system, which is designed to protect the human body from disease.

The immune system normally functions by producing special cells and antibodies that attack bacteria, viruses, and other foreign substances in the body. Sometimes, however, the system breaks down and begins destroying the body's own healthy cells. Diseases resulting from such malfunctions are called *autoimmune* diseases, and there is some evidence that Alzheimer's may be among them.

One strong indication of this is the presence of a protein called *amyloid* within the plaques that develop in the brains of Alzheimer's victims. This same substance has been found in cells destroyed by diseases that are known to be of the autoimmune variety. Like Alzheimer's disease, many of these diseases are particularly common among older people. This combination of facts has led researchers to look for other similarities between Alzheimer's disease and illnesses caused by disorders in the immune system.

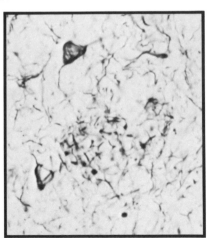

The plaques that develop within the brain cells of Alzheimer's victims contain a protein called amyloid. This same substance is found in cells destroyed by some autoimmune diseases.

A More Hopeful Future

With research being conducted in so many different areas, scientists are hopeful that a major discovery concerning the cause of Alzheimer's disease will be made soon. No one expects, however, that the solution to the puzzle will be a simple one. Like many major illnesses, Alzheimer's disease probably results from a combination of factors rather than a single, simple cause.

For example, certain people may inherit a set of genes that makes them vulnerable to Alzheimer's disease rather than causing the disease itself. When these people are exposed to some other agent, perhaps a slow-acting virus, they would be more likely to develop the disease than those with a different genetic heritage. Other even more complicated combinations of factors could be responsible for producing the destructive symptoms of Alzheimer's disease.

Research into the causes of Alzheimer's disease is vitally important not only to the world of science but also to the victims of the disease and to their families. Only by knowing something about the factors that produce the illness will it be possible to develop effective treatments to control its symptoms. Eventually such knowledge may make it possible to eradicate the disease completely.

Much remains to be learned before we can achieve any of these goals, but significant progress has been made in some areas. As we have seen, advances in our knowledge of the brain's chemical circuits have allowed researchers to pinpoint a possible source of the cell damage that occurs in Alzheimer's disease. In the area of diagnosis, new kinds of equipment and techniques are making it easier to recognize the disease. The CAT scan, mentioned earlier, has proved helpful in this area. A newer scanning technique, the *PET scan,* has been even more useful in diagnosing Alzheimer's disease.

PET stands for "Positron-Emission Tomography," a revolutionary method of revealing the actual operation of a living brain. This technique makes use of radioactive materials to show the functioning of cells in different areas of the brain.

A patient who is to receive a PET scan is usually injected with a glucose solution that contains radioactive particles called positrons. Glucose, a form of sugar, is the brain's main source of energy. When brain cells are at work, receiving signals and transmitting information, they use large amounts of glucose. The PET scanner is able to record the activity of the cells by measuring the radioactive emissions of the positrons in the glucose. The more activity in a particular area of the brain, the more positron emissions will be recorded in that area.

Like a CAT scan, a PET scan uses a computer to produce cross-section images, or tomographs, of the brain based on the readings that it makes. The images portray in vivid colors the areas where cell activity is

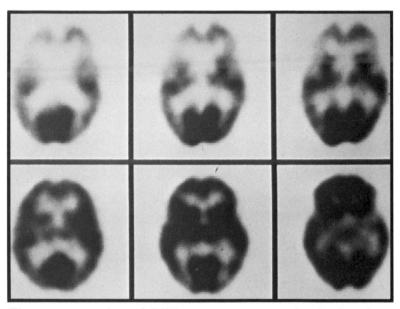

These two series of PET scans compare the brain of an Alzheimer victim (top) with that of a normal person of the same age (bottom). The dark areas in the scans reveal the parts of the brains where cells are active. As you can see, the brain of the Alzheimer victim shows less activity than that of the unaffected person.

taking place. They also pinpoint regions where cells are underactive. In Alzheimer's victims, the cells in the cortex, particularly in the frontal and parietal lobes, show less activity than in a normal brain. These readings correspond to the kind of cell damage usually revealed in an autopsy on an Alzheimer's victim. The regions of low cell activity seem to be those most severely damaged by the lesions of the disease.

PET scanning can be a valuable tool in diagnosing Alzhemier's disease because it makes it possible to identify the illness in an early stage of its development. If effective treatments for the disease are eventually discovered, early diagnosis will mean that victims could be helped before damage to their brains became widespread. Today, early diagnosis allows scientists to study all the stages of the illness and learn as much as possible about its development.

Another revolutionary medical technique that may eventually be enlisted in the war against Alzheimer's disease is *Magnetic Resonance Imaging (MRI)*. Like PET scanning, MRI is capable of producing detailed images of a living brain. This technique makes use of the natural magnetic properties of some of the atoms in the body, including hydrogen and phosphorus. When subjected to a powerful magnetic force from outside the body, these atoms respond in certain recognizable ways. By measuring and evaluating the responses, the MRI scanner can detect the existence of abnormal tissue in the body's organs, including the brain. Like the PET scanner, it can also reveal some of the chemical activities taking place in brain cells.

Magnetic Resonance Imaging is a new technique whose potential is still being explored by scientists. Many believe, however, that it holds great promise as a safe and practical diagnostic tool because, unlike CAT and PET scanning, it does not require the use of radiation or radioactive materials.

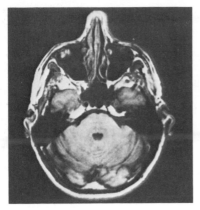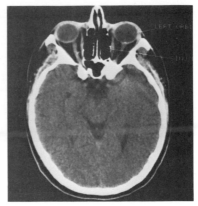

Above: A scan produced by Magnetic Resonance Imaging (left) gives a much more detailed picture of the brain than a CAT scan (right). *Below:* To create its images, an MRI scanner uses a magnetic force 25,000 times more powerful than the earth's magnetic field. This revolutionary imaging technique shows great promise as a research and diagnostic tool in the study of Alzheimer's disease.

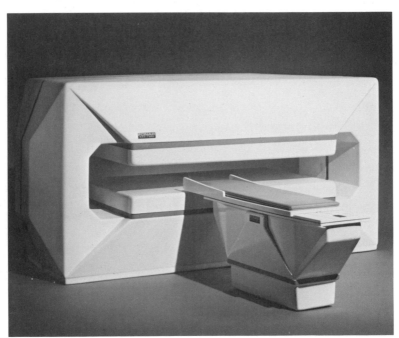

At the present time, both MRI and PET scanning are used primarily for research rather than for day-to-day diagnosis. Not many medical institutions can afford the expensive equipment these techniques require, which, in the case of PET scanning, includes a cyclotron for the production of radioactive materials. Researchers, however, are making good use of these exciting medical tools in their search for the causes of Alzheimer's disease. In the future, PET and MRI scanning may be available for an even wider range of uses.

SHARING THE BURDEN

What does the future hold for victims of Alzheimer's disease and their families? If scientists do not discover an effective treatment for the illness, how will future generations deal with the tremendous medical, personal, and social problems that it will cause?

Based on present statistics, we know that Alzheimer's disease will be much more common in 20 or 30 years than it is today. The continued growth of the elderly population in North America and in some other parts of the world means that there will be many more potential victims of this deadly disease that usually strikes people over the age of 60.

The trend toward an older population is particularly noticeable in the United States. In 1983, for the first time in the country's history, there were more Americans over 65 than there were teenagers. As this trend

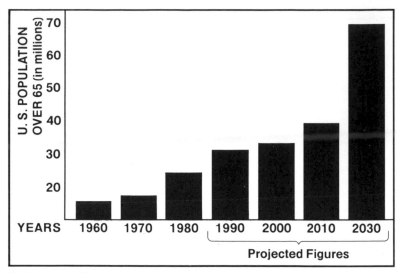

This graph illustrates the dramatic increase in the older population that is expected to take place in the United States during the coming years. As the number of elderly people grows, more and more cases of Alzheimer's disease are bound to occur.

continues, more and more cases of Alzheimer's disease are bound to occur. Unless an effective treatment for the disease is developed, the task of providing adequate care for the millions of helpless victims will be enormous.

In the future, as now, the primary caregivers will probably be the families of Alzheimer's victims. But what about people who, unlike Sarah, do not have close and loving families with adequate resources to see them through the tragic course of their illness? Andrew's story shows what can happen to such a victim:

After his wife died and he retired from his job at the post office, 65-year-old Andrew moved to a trailer park.

He had no children, and his other relatives were scattered over the country. Andrew had no close friends. For the most part, he was content to live alone and see other people only when he felt like it.

Because Andrew was so isolated, no one knew him well enough to notice when he began to show early signs of Alzheimer's disease. His cousins were a little surprised when they didn't hear from him at the holidays, but they were busy with their own lives and did not try to find out what was wrong. Andrew's neighbors noticed that he no longer dressed neatly and that his yard was a mess. None of them had lived in the trailer park for very long, however, and each thought that someone else should check and see if Andrew needed help

Andrew went on in this way for about two years. As his illness progressed, he had trouble sleeping at night, and he sometimes wandered around outside. One morning, a family living a few blocks from his home found him sleeping under a tree in their backyard. He seemed very confused and could not tell them where he lived.

The family called the police, who quickly realized that Andrew was ill and took him to the emergency room at the hospital. A nurse in the emergency room got Andrew to tell her his name and looked up his address and phone number in the telephone book. When no relatives or close friends could be located, he was admitted to the hospital.

After Andrew's illness was diagnosed as Alzheimer's disease, the hospital was faced with a problem. Andrew could not be helped by further medical treatment, yet he was clearly too sick to be sent home alone. A social worker was assigned to his case, and with a little detective work, she tracked down his cousins and other relatives. None of them was able to care for Andrew, however, so the problem of where he should live was still not solved.

Andrew's difficulties were made worse by his financial situation. His health insurance would pay for hospital treatment but not for long-term care in a nursing home, which was what Andrew really needed. He could not afford to pay for a nursing home himself, but because he owned some property and had a small pension, he did not qualify for government assistance.

Finally, for lack of a better solution, the social worker arranged to have Andrew transferred to the state mental hospital. The hospital, which was understaffed and crowded with seriously disturbed patients, was not a good place for Andrew. Even though he was confused, he was alert enough to miss his home and to be upset by the atmosphere of the institution. Andrew demanded to be released from the hospital, but the doctors on the staff felt that he was not capable of living on his own. They arranged to have a court hearing to decide if Andrew could be kept against his will. The judge ruled that this was justified under the circumstances.

Several months later, a second court hearing was held, resulting in the appointment of a legal guardian for Andrew, who was considered no longer capable of making his own decisions. The guardian arranged to sell Andrew's trailer, using the money to pay for a place in a nursing home. When the money was used up, the guardian applied for government aid to pay for Andrew's care. With this assistance, Andrew was able to stay in the nursing home until his death five years later.

Andrew was particularly unfortunate because he had to face Alzheimer's disease alone, without the support of relatives who could provide care or assist him in his illness. Even victims with close and supportive families, however, may experience some of the same problems that Andrew did. Many families lack the financial resources to pay for the care of their demented relatives. Providing care for a permanently demented person, either in a private home or in an institution, is very expensive, and assistance is not easy to obtain.

Today, many private medical insurance plans do not pay for the kind of care needed by demented patients. The federal Medicare program, designed to help older people with medical expenses, usually applies only to "skilled care," that given by a registered nurse or a licensed practical nurse. Since most victims of Alzheimer's disease do not require skilled nursing care, they do not often qualify for the Medicare program.

Another federal program, Medicaid, does cover such "custodial" care, but it can be used only by those who cannot afford to pay themselves. Like Andrew, many victims have to give up almost everything they own to qualify for this program.

If the future brings with it an epidemic of Alzheimer's disease, as researchers fear it will, then the problem of providing adequate care will become acute. Many experts believe that we must begin planning now to make sure that families of victims will be able to get the financial assistance they will need. They are also concerned about the availability of nursing homes and other facilities capable of taking care of large numbers of victims in the sad, final stage of the disease.

Today there are several organizations that are concerned not only with future victims of Alzheimer's disease but also with those who are now suffering from the illness. The most important is a group called the Alzheimer's Disease and Related Disorders Association (ADRDA). Made up primarily of the families of Alzheimer's victims, the association helps its members to fulfill their difficult roles as guardians and caretakers. It holds meetings at which members talk about their experiences and share practical advice about medical treatment and ways of dealing with demented relatives. In addition to acting as a support group for families of victims, ADRDA sponsors research on Alzheimer's disease and attempts to educate the general public about this frightening illness.

During a therapy session for Alzheimer's victims held at the Burke Rehabilitation Center in White Plains, New York, program coordinator John Panella reintroduces a participant, Doris Miller, to other group members. Therapy programs such as this one are designed to help people in the early stages of Alzheimer's disease to deal with memory loss and confusion.

Much of what we know today about Alzheimer's disease is frightening and discouraging, but there are some rays of hope in the generally bleak picture. The recognition that severe confusion and memory loss in older people are symptoms of a disease and not natural consequences of aging is a promising sign for the future. A disease can be cured or at least treated, whereas "senility" can only be accepted and lived with.

If the cause of Alzheimer's disease is eventually discovered and an effective treatment developed, then millions of older people will be able to spend the final years of their lives mentally alert, independent, and whole. Until that day comes, victims of the disease and their families deserve our understanding and deepest sympathy. They are carrying a very heavy burden.

GLOSSARY

adrenergic (ad-reh-NUHR-jik) brain circuits—groups of neurons that use norepinethrine (NE) as their primary neurotransmitter. In some victims of Alzheimer's disease, these circuits are abnormal.

amygdala (uh-MIG-duh-luh)—a structure in the limbic system involved in the transformation of recent memories into long-term memories

amyloid (am-eh-LOID)—a protein substance found within the plaques caused by Alzheimer's disease. This same substance appears in cells destroyed by some auto-immune diseases.

association cortex—parts of the frontal, temporal, and parietal lobes that seem to control the process of thinking, planning, and retaining memories

autoimmune diseases—diseases caused by malfunctions in the body's immune system

axon (AK-sahn)—a long, tail-like structure that extends from the body of a neuron and transmits nerve impulses to other neurons

brain peptides (PEP-tides)—a group of neurotransmitters, including somatostatin and vasopressin, that may be involved in the development of Alzheimer's disease

cerebral (seh-REE-bruhl) cortex—the thin, wrinkled outer layer of the cerebrum, where most higher brain functions take place

cholinergic (ko-leh-NUHR-jik) brain circuits—groups of neurons that use acetylcholine as their primary neuro-transmitter. In some Alzheimer's victims, these circuits are abnormal.

circuits—groups of neurons connected to each other by a particular neurotransmitter

Computerized Axial Tomography (CAT)—a special x-ray technique that produces images of the soft tissue of the body

dementia (di-MEN-chuh)—a mental condition characterized by such symptoms as confusion, memory loss, and irrational behavior

dementing illnesses—illnesses such as Alzheimer's disease whose victims suffer from dementia

dendrites (DEN-drites)—the thin, branching structures that extend from the cell body of a neuron and receive nerve impulses from other neurons

frontal lobes (LOHBES)—the sections of the cerebrum that occupy the front part of the skull, under the frontal bones

glial (GLEE-uhl) cells—brain cells that support and nourish the neurons

hippocampus (hip-eh-KAM-pus)—a structure in the limbic system involved in the transformation of recent memories into long-term memories. The name comes from the Greek word for "seahorse," referring to the unusual shape of this brain structure.

incontinence (in-KAHN-teh-nance)—inability to control urination and bowel movements

lesions (LEE-zhuns)—abnormal changes in the brain cells of Alzheimer's victims

limbic system—a group of brain structures involved in the control of emotions and memory

long-term memory—the faculty of retaining information in the brain for long periods of time

Magnetic Resonance Imaging (MRI)—a medical technique that produces detailed images of the body through the use of a powerful magnetic force

neuron (NYU-ron)—a nerve cell

neurofibrillary (nyur-oh-FIB-ri-lar-ee) tangles—twisted threads of protein found in brain cells destroyed by Alzheimer's disease

neurotransmitters (nyur-oh-TRANS-mit-uhrs)—chemicals that cross the synaptic cleft between neurons, transmitting nerve impulses from one cell to another

occipital (ahk-SIP-uh-tuhl) lobes—the back sections of the cerebrum, located under the occipital bones of the skull

parietal (peh-RI-uh-tuhl) lobes—the middle sections of the cerebrum, located under the parietal bones of the skull

plaques (PLAKS)—patches of dead cells found in the brains of Alzheimer's victims

Positron-emission Tomography (PET)—a medical technique that uses radioactive material to produce images of brain cells in action

senility (si-NIL-ih-tee)—a loss of mental ability frequently considered as a normal part of aging. Today, many scientists believe that this condition is caused by specific illnesses like Alzheimer's disease.

short-term memory—the faculty of retaining information in the brain for short periods of time

stroke—an interruption in the supply of blood to the brain

synaptic (sih-NAP-tik) cleft—the space that separates the axon of one neuron from the dendrites of another neuron

temporal lobes—the sections of the cerebrum located at the sides of the head, under the temporal bones of the skull

terminal branches—the branching structures at the end of a neuron's axon

INDEX

If you would like to find out more about Alzheimer's disease, the Alzheimer's Disease and Related Disorders Association (ADRDA) is a good source of information. Its national headquarters is located at 360 North Michigan Avenue, Chicago, Illinois 60601.

I'VE LOST A KINGDOM

Many articles about Alzheimer's disease have appeared in recent years. One unusual treatment can be found in the December 1984 issue of the *Journal of the American Geriatrics Society.* "I've Lost a Kingdom: A Victim's Remarks on Alzheimer's Disease" presents the thoughts and feelings of Dr. Marguerite Rush Lerner, a victim in the early stages of Alzheimer's disease. The remarks listed below and the quotations used as chapter headings were taken from this source.

I have a neurological problem. Who needs it? No one.

I can't tell you how terrible things have been for me—to go from health to nothing.

Nobody likes me. I don't like myself either.

I used to be a physician. I used to drive a car. What do I want? I don't want to be here.

I know that I am not functioning as a mother or a spouse. You have to do all the work.

Am I always going to be sick? It would be nice if someone could help me.

I don't sing anymore. I probably won't sing again.

I am afraid of everything.

I shouldn't be here. I am just waiting until I die.

All I do is nothing.

Look how nice these boys are—and what a terrible mother. How did I get this way? I must have taken a wrong turn.

You need a new wife. This one is no good anymore.

I think that I am getting better and all the time I am getting worse.

The days go so slow for me.

No one knows my name anymore—because I am nothing.

I've lost everything—typing and writing. I don't have any skills. All I do is eat. I have to go away. I can't read my own writing.

I've had a good life—a successful marriage—good children—a good career. Now there is nothing for me. I've lived too long.

It was so much fun with the students when I was a teacher.

It is hard when one becomes obsolete.

I've lost a kingdom.

I wish I were a little girl again.